LLC

The Ultimate Guide to Forming Your LLC in 10 Simple Steps

Elliot J. Smith

Contents

Introduction

I want to thank you and congratulate you for downloading the book *LLC: 10 Steps to Forming Your LLC*.

This book contains proven steps and strategies for forming your very own LLC.

Here's an inescapable fact: you will need to understand and follow the laws and rules created by the state in which you live to create a successful LLC.

If you do not have a thorough understanding of how an LLC works, you will not be successful.

It's time for you to become an amazing LLC owner.

Chapter 1

Limited Liability Company Fundamentals

The LLC, or limited liability company, is fairly new in the United States, with Wyoming being the first state to enact LLC legislation in 1977. Florida followed suit in 1982, but other states had little incentive to enact such legislation because it was unclear how the IRS would treat an LLC in terms of taxes: as a corporation or a partnership. It wasn't until 1988 that the IRS made a ruling allowing an LLC in Wyoming to be treated as a partnership. This meant that taxable profits and losses would flow through the owners; unlike with a traditional corporation, an LLC would not be taxed as a separate organization.

After the 1988 ruling, nearly every state enacted an LLC statute, making the LLC a common and widely recognized business form. State law governs the creation of an LLC, meaning the people who want to form an LLC must file with the appropriate state authority, which is most often the secretary of state. Most states also require the filing of articles of organization; these are public documents very similar to articles of incorporation. The articles of organization must be filed for an LLC to be a legal entity, and the LLC generally comes into existence when the articles are filed and the necessary fees are paid.

The minimum requirements for the articles of organization vary according to the state, but generally, they must include the name of the LLC, the name of the person or people creating the LLC, the LLC's duration, and the name of the LLC's registered agent. It is important to know exactly what your state requires when you file, as this will streamline the process and save time. For instance, in addition to the previously mentioned items, some states require the LLC's business purpose, management plan, and membership structure. Every state requires that a business name include words or phrases that will identify it as an LLC, but what is acceptable varies by state, as some will simply allow an abbreviation while others prefer it to be spelled out completely.

Many people find the limited liability part of an LLC to be the most appealing quality and it is this trait that increased the LLC's popularity. Basically, LLC members are protected from personal liability for business claims and debts. Should the business be unable to pay a creditor, like a landlord, lender, or supplier, the creditor cannot legally come after the member's personal possessions, such as their car or home. Only LLC assets are used to pay off business debts, meaning that LLC members risk only losing the money they have invested in the business.

LLC Member Types:

The owner or owners of an LLC are called members. Unlike a corporation, each member is an owner of the company; there are no owners' shares. There are two types of LLC memberships:

1. Single-Member-LLC

2. Multiple-Member-LLC

The only difference between the two types of memberships is in the way they are taxed. A single-member-LLC is taxed as a sole proprietorship, which means that the information about the LLC's income and expenses comes from one owner or member's personal tax statement. For a multiple-member-LLC, the individual members pay taxes based on their share of ownership; this is also how partnerships are taxed.

There can be a non-manager member and a manager member; this is exactly as it sounds. A manager member acts on behalf of the company to make decisions during the daily operations of the business. There can be more than one managing member if need be. A non-managing member can still vote when needed but is not required to be present for daily business operations unless there are extenuating circumstances. Most smaller LLCs and single-member LLCs are member-managed because the cost to do so is cheaper. This can be incredibly helpful during the formation phase when there are no profits to be had yet.

Operating Agreement

An LLC operating agreement outlines the structure of the company, including the financial and working relationships. Each member's percentage of ownership is detailed in the operating agreement, as are how the profits and losses are divided and each member's responsibilities in terms of the business itself. Not every state requires an operating agreement, but most would agree that it is foolish to run a multi-member LLC without one because it is used for so many things. For instance, many disagreements can be prevented with a well-made operations agreement because the dynamics will be spelled out for the members. Another reason to have an operations agreement is to protect yourself, as it will ensure that the courts respect the limited personal liability. Without an operations agreement, it could be assumed that the LLC is actually either a partnership or a sole proprietorship. A formal operating agreement will lend credibility to your LLC's separate existence should you ever need to prove it.

A good operating agreement will be very detailed and outline each person's responsibilities and all the inner workings of the business. The operating agreement should leave very few questions unanswered, so people will know going in what they should expect out of their involvement.

Ideally, each member should receive a copy of the operating agreement so if questions do arise, one can easily check to see if the answer is already there. The operating agreement must be signed by every member of the LLC for it to be enforced. In addition, it is much easier to tweak the operating agreement as it is being drafted than once it is finished and being enforced.

Alliances

Businesses and companies work together to form an alliance to achieve mutually beneficial objectives. These companies can share information, resources, and capabilities to achieve these goals. Alliances mean that a company can learn from and obtain information about another company's innovations without having to spend money on research and development. Companies have also achieved the same results through acquisitions, but alliances are more cost effective.

A good way to think of an alliance is as two companies that are sharing for the common good. Maybe they are in an area with limited resources and an alliance saves them money. Another reason for an alliance is that each company produces something that complements the other, so it makes fiscal sense for them to be associated in one way or another. Imagine that one company makes printers while the other company makes ink. They are fine separately, but their products complement each other so well that it makes sense for them to form an alliance.

Management

An LLC can be a manager-managed company, which is when the members own the company but choose not to be the manager. Instead, an outside employee who is not a member of the LLC is hired to manage the company. On the other hand, one or more of the members can be a managing member, in which case they are present for and run the company's day-to-day business. Many LLCs are created with a managing member structure in mind, mostly for financial reasons, because it is cheaper than hiring an employee. A managing member has the power to contract on behalf of the company, participates in daily issues, and holds an ownership interest in the company.

Unlike non-managing members, a managing member can act as an agent of the company and can sell and buy products and property based on the normal course of business. Managing members can also hire and fire employees, direct the operations of the company, and even bind the company by participating in contracts on its behalf. Non-managing members do not act as agents of the company. Their authority is limited and generally explained in the operations agreement. The limited liability protects all members from torts committed by employees and each other. However, it will not protect any member for their own torts either inside or outside the ordinary course of business. This means that because a managing member is more involved in the operations of the business, their activities could expose them to a higher liability than a non-managing member.

Taxes

An LLC is not considered a separate tax entity like a corporation is. It is what the IRS calls a "pass-through entity," similar to a sole proprietorship or a partnership. This means that all the losses and profits "pass through" the business itself to the members, who then report the information on their own personal tax returns. The LLC itself is not required to pay income taxes, but some states do require a tax.

The IRS treats a single-member LLC as a sole proprietorship, which means that the sole owner of the LLC must report all profits and losses on their own tax returns. Even if the owner leaves profits in a business bank account for things such as expanding the business or future expenses, at the end of the year they will be responsible for paying taxes on that money.

Multi-member LLCs are treated as a partnership when it comes to taxes. Each LLC owner pays taxes based on their lawful share of the profits. Each member's share of profits and losses, or a distributive share, is laid out in the LLC's operating agreement. A member's distributive share is usually in proportion to their percentage of interest in the company. If the distributive shares are going to be divided in a way that is not in proportion to interest in the company, this is called "special allocation.

No matter how the shares are divided, the IRS assumes that each LLC member receives their entire distributive share each year. This means that each member must pay taxes based on their distributive shares regardless of whether the LLC actually gives them the money. The reason for this rule is that if the members leave profits in an account, each member is still responsible for paying taxes on the money in the account based on their distributive shares even though they did not physically receive the money.

It is also a common misconception that LLCs will be small. That is not always the case. For instance, the cookie company Mrs. Fields LLC is one of the best-known. The LLC was founded in Utah in 2004 and is famous for its brownies, cookies, cakes, bagels, and smoothies. Most companies that start out as an LLC do not remain that way when they become larger simply because of the issues that can arise with more members.

Chapter 2

LLC Member Rights and Responsibilities

Being involved in an LLC can be very beneficial in business because of investment and security, but many people do not know the specific responsibilities they have as a member of an LLC. Shareholders of a company have obligations, just as a member of an LLC does, but with those obligations come special rights such as sharing in the profits. Depending on the agreement of members, you may be asked to participate in the daily operations of the business. Other times you might be needed to make important decisions with the other members.

It is important to remember the flexibility that an LLC gives its members. Even though most members became members by investing money, this is not the only method. It is possible to become a member just like any other member by contributing assets when the LLC is forming. Some people become members by contributing professional expertise or valuable property. Sometimes promissory notes are accepted so long as the other members agree to allow it. There are no restrictions when it comes to what a member must contribute to be a founding member. Some states do have age requirements, so not anyone can be a member, but again, this will not be an issue in some states.

If done properly, when you want to know how admission to your LLC works, all it will take is a look at the operations agreement. Generally, the agreement will mention that the other members must all agree with the decision of whether to allow entrance of a new member. The agreement should also include stipulations about the contribution a potential member must provide, such as the amount, form, size, or magnitude, depending on its form. Also, the operating agreement should include the terms of expulsion or suspension in regards to existing members. If your LLC's operating agreement does not include this information, you are expected to use the LLC act.

Main Rights as a Member

Finances – Most people choose to become a member in an LLC because they know that with ownership interest comes a share of the company profits. In addition, you have the right to participate in the distribution of tangible assets. This is still true regardless of whether the business is an ongoing concern or planning to end.

It is also important to remember that the amount of your profit sharing will be outlined in the operating agreement. If the operating agreement does not have a detailed explanation of this, it is your responsibility to abide by the state laws that include default standard criteria. It is definitely in your best interest to include this in the operating agreement, though, because default laws are not going to benefit anyone. If you have control of profit sharing, you know how to split it so that it remains fair.

Voting – Each member has the right to vote on nearly every facet of the business, but only if the LLC is a member-managed company. Some LLCs have different forms of membership. The stipulations should be broken down in the operating agreement. One of these stipulations might include a list of members who are not eligible or required to vote. Should this be the case, these members will simply not vote when the time arises.

If your LLC is or will be managed by someone who is not a member but, instead, a hired employee, other members' voting abilities will be limited to the most important issues, such as admission of new members, matters involving potential mergers, amendments to the already existing operating agreement, amendments to the articles of organization, dissolution, and any other pressing matters. Also, when circumstances arise with respect to engaging or terminating the services of the company, members will have the ability to vote; managers take care of the business operations and the members have no say.

Many states require that an LLC keep specific records and that those records be readily available for members to inspect at any time. These basic records generally include:

- Names of current members

- Addresses of current members

- Copies of the three most recent consecutive years' tax returns, including both federal and state, if applicable

- An updated copy of the operating agreement

- Financial statements of the LLC, preferably the three most recent consecutive years

Even states that do not necessarily require that an LLC maintain records for inspection by members will stress the importance of this to ensure that members know exactly what is expected of them and will be better able to perform to the best of their abilities. In situations in which the operating agreement is too vague or does not include the necessary information, the default is the LLC statute.

Right to Dissent

This right refers to a member's being able to refuse acceptance of a form of ownership for which they did not sign up. Basically, this means that the character of the interest a member has in the company can't be changed. For instance, imagine you are involved with an LLC that entered a merger agreement with a separate company without consulting with you. The LLC would not have your agreement to the move. At that point, you have the right to demand that the LLC buy back your personal interest in the company at a reasonable value.

Another example of this would be if the company sold its assets and completely changed the nature of the company with respect to the nature of the original LLC for which you signed up. It is important to remember, too, that not all states detail in their acts the right to dissent, while other states indicate that this issue should be outlined in detail in the operating agreement.

Derivative Suit

A derivative suit means that you can initiate a suit against people either within or outside the organization who are tampering with the company itself. This includes behavior that would put it at a disadvantage or in jeopardy. The suit would be made on behalf of the LLC, and if the court were to rule in your favor, it would mean that the LLC had won. Therefore, any damages awarded would go to the business itself and not the members.

Valid Suit

These are the conditions that must be filled for a successful suit:

You must have been a member of the LLC when the damages were inflicted upon the company.

You must have made decent attempts to get the company itself to sue, but ultimately failed to do so.

In some states, the LLC act does not give members the right to a derivative suit. If you find yourself in this position, there is no reason to hesitate about fighting for your company. Your state laws might allow you to sue under common law, but if that is still not an option, continue with the suit and let the courts of law decide how they should handle the situation in the interest of your company.

Compensation

If you decided upon a member-managed LLC, you are all required to participate in the affairs of the company. However, if you or one of the other members actively runs the daily operations of the business on behalf of the other members, you or the acting managing member has the right to be compensated either financially or in a manner that provides ongoing motivation. These are more of the stipulations that should be included in the operating agreement.

Disassociation

Members have the right to leave an LLC at any time, but only if the procedure in the operating agreement is properly followed. Sometimes if someone were to leave the LLC without following the rules or procedures in the operating agreement, they can be slapped with liability against the company.

Obligations

If you are the active managing member of an LLC, you are obligated to take part in running its affairs. However, once the LLC is formed and if the members realize that no one is suitable as a manager, it is possible to amend the operating agreement; so long as all members agree, an outside manager may be hired.

The operating agreement will also explain how the profits and any other benefits will be distributed among the members. One of the obligations of any member, but especially for the managing member, is to stick to this. Again, the flexibility of an LLC means that changes can be made if necessary as long as all members agree. Should a change in the distribution be required, this can also be altered in the operating agreement. However, be sure to check state laws because some have stipulations. If there is the use of special allocation, the IRS must be notified as well; otherwise, members will be personally liable.

Managing members of an LLC must be especially careful not to breach fiduciary duties to the company. They must also follow and respect the requirements and provisions of the operating agreement. This holds true for those who have left an LLC that contains a non-compete clause in the operating agreement. The previous member has a fiduciary duty to not slander or try to harm the business.

The extent of a member's interest in the company and the distributive shares spelled out in the operating agreement include losses in addition to profits. This means that if the company is dissolved and its assets liquidated, members suffer losses too; therefore, generally they cannot expect the full contribution if the company's liabilities surpass its assets.

Chapter 3

Why an LLC?

There are many positives to an LLC, and this structure has been ideal for many businesses. However, they are not without their limitations; what works for one business might not be the best fit for another. Hopefully, this information will help you decide whether an LLC is a correct direction and path for you to take.

Business Classifications

C Corporation – This is a business entity that is subject to federal income tax, but its shareholders are not subject to tax unless they have collected dividends, salaries, or distributions.

S Corporation – This type of business is not subject to federal income tax. Instead, the company's shareholders are responsible for paying federal income tax on the taxable portion of the profits.

LLC – Like S Corporations, LLCs are treated as pass-through entities by the IRS unless they choose to be taxed as a corporation. The IRS treats LLCs as sole proprietorships for tax purposes, or as partnerships if they are multi-member LLCs, yet still with the legal liability shield.

Sole Proprietorship/Partnership – Both are cheap and easy to create, but they do not offer liability protection. All profits are treated as personal and taxable income.

Despite your revolutionary product or your need to expand your business, an LLC format might be an obstacle in finding investors. These issues are most predominant in the startup sectors, in which companies might go through several rounds of reinvestment and financing.

This is nothing to take personally; investors just tend to avoid any entity-based taxation. They do this for their own best interests because it can complicate things for them, resulting in them being taxed on allocation even if they never received distributions. Investors also prefer "easy-in, easy-out" investments, and LLCs are constructed contractually instead of being based on statutes, as is the case with corporations. Therefore, each investment opportunity can be extremely different based on what the operations agreement says.

Some investors also are simply unable to invest in an LLC. For example, venture funds are unable to invest in an LLC or other pass-through entities because they usually have tax-exempt partners. If they were to invest in an LLC, they would be considered a member and, come time for taxes, they would no longer be exempt because they would be responsible for paying based on their interest in the company.

The argument could be made that successful investors have turned their investment practices into an art. They know that to enhance their investments, they must reinvest in the companies in their portfolio. Many operating agreements have stipulations for how profits will be distributed and how much of them will remain in the business; situations like this can hinder reinvestment and be disadvantageous to profitable and healthy investment.

Many investors are not as familiar with the way an LLC works as compared to a more traditional corporation. LLCs are relatively new compared to corporations and therefore they have a much less uniform structure. Investments are often controlled risks, and when placing a wager, it is better to bet on what you understand rather than give money to something you might not fully comprehend.

All of this means that LLCs are usually poor options for serious and professional investors. It is possible to create an operating agreement that is more traditional and enticing to investors, but many will still overlook it without a second thought. Don't let this dissuade you; it is still possible to find investors, but just know that many investors will be less likely to give money to an LLC.

Taxation

Venture firms with tax-exempt partners will stay away from any pass-through entities, but there are still more tax implications that could dissuade a potential investor. For instance, the risk of tax liability exists in some states. Imagine that a passive investor who lives in New York invests a large amount of money in his friend's food truck, The Tiki Shrimp Food Truck LLC, in California. When taxes are filed, the friend in New York must file a Form K-1 in the state of California in addition to New York taxes. This happens even to those who are passive investors.

Allotment – not distribution – is taxed. This means that the investor in New York could owe taxes based on his share of the company even if he did not receive a share of the profits. Professional investors make their money from the benefits of their investments, so this type of risk is just that appealing to a professional investor. This also happens to alien investors or investors from other countries.

The complex way that LLCs are taxed combined with the other obstacles for investors makes buying stock in a C Corp seem much more convenient and beneficial. When abiding by the tax implications and investment barriers connected to LLCs, raising capital can come with its own unique set of challenges. Let's assume that you have succeeded in finding a pool of investors. With a C Corp, there is a very strict structure that simplifies the process of raising rounds of capital. However, no such guidelines exist for an LLC; in the end, your investors will still be fixed with tax obligations on their investments the following year.

Concerns for Members

LLCs can offer advantages over the more traditional sole proprietorship entity structure, but these advantages do not come without a cost. LLCs are created with contracts instead of statutes, which is why they are sometimes called "contract creatures." This also means that LLCs have more complexity and variability than other entities. An LLC is more free form, which means that most its structure comes from contracts and its operating agreement. These contracts are very important to the business and, if done well, can be costly, complex, and even difficult to create.

Although an LLC can give its members a lot of control over how they are operated, getting the details wrong can have negative long-term effects. This can be a liability for both the members and the investors. The modes of operation can vary greatly from one LLC to another.

Multi-member LLCs are taxed as partnerships, which can make equity compensation fairly difficult. This is due to a lack of statutory guidelines dealing with equity compensation within an LLC. The process can be incredibly complex and time consuming because LLCs are forced to "book up" or adjust capital accounts for every instance of equity sharing.

If it is not immediately obvious which entity structure would work best for you, it would be beneficial to schedule an appointment with a CPA. Using their expertise, a professional can guide you and provide advice about making the best decision, one that works for you and your business.

An LLC might be the right fit for you if:

- Your startup company foresees losses for at least two years and you would rather deal with those losses between yourself and the other members.

- You might decide to own real estate.

- You like the idea of sharing profits among members.

- Management flexibility is important to you.

- You do not want to use the traditional accrual method and you appreciate options when it comes to accounting.

- You would like to minimize formalities, meaning you can pick and choose when and if meetings are held based on your needs, not because of directors and shareholders.

This list should help when you are deciding which structure works best for you. However, and this cannot be said enough, not all states are the same. Make sure your state will let you form a single-member LLC if that is your goal. LLCs have fewer rules and enjoy more flexibility, but they are young, which means that they are not as understood and accepted as are other companies. There are many successful LLCs, though, so if you truly think that this is the best route for you, it is possible to make the system work. Something as complex as this requires a great deal of patience. A guide later in this book will break down the steps of forming an LLC.

Chapter 4

Mistakes to Avoid When Forming an LLC

Even though LLCs are relatively young in the business world, there are still rules to follow during the formation phase. The most critical aspect is the operating agreement. If the operating agreement is detailed and specific, it will create a foundation that will lead to success. The formation of an LLC is a complex process, and there are many things you can either do or not do to make your life easier or more stressful. This list is based on errors that others have made, so you can learn from other people's mistakes.

Common Mistakes

Legal Assistance – Many people fail to seek legal help, especially during the formation phase of their

LLC. However, legal help can prevent many issues that you could possibly face down the line. A study conducted by LegalShield found that 60 percent of small businesses suffered a significant legal event within the previous two years, but only half of them sought help from a lawyer. This would mean that there are more than three million legally untrained business owners who think it is a good idea to do their own legal work. One of the best ways to prevent situations like this is to seek legal assistance when you think you need it.

Disclose – Be honest with your lawyer and the other members of the LLC. Tell them everything; if you don't, you are setting yourself up for failure. Even if something seems unimportant, if it could have ramifications for the business, speak up. For instance, friends were starting a business in a state that required all principles and members to be without a criminal record. Well into the process, after money and time had been spent on getting a business license, the state denied the request. One of the members had failed to mention that he had a prior conviction for fraud and embezzlement. This was a major setback that cost everyone time and money – and, in this case, probably caused humiliation.

Complete Documents – This seems like common sense, but it is one of the most common mistakes people make. Make sure all documents are signed, dated, initialed, copied, and distributed appropriately to all members. Obviously, the most important of these documents is the operating agreement, so make sure it is signed by each member. Also, make sure each member has a copy of the completed, signed document. In addition, it would be beneficial for you to have the documents looked over by an attorney, to make sure everything is coherent and as it should be. This is the kind of thing you want to find out early and not have to pay for down the road.

Cheap Shortcuts – Occurrences of this trap are growing because so many different documents can easily be found on the internet. These legal documents are not tailored to specific needs. Recently a young entrepreneur wanted to add two new members to her online business. She had already filed the LLC paperwork using free documents she found online. She wanted the process to be as easy and cheap as possible, but she finally thought better of it and decided to seek a professional to check out everything. Come to find out, her documents contained a provision that voting would be based on head count, not on a percentage of ownership like she had desired. If someone had not looked over her documents, she would not have had majority control over her company as she initially wanted.

Protect Yourself – Sometimes protecting intellectual property can be tricky. For a brand-new concept, few bulletproof legal safeguards exist. When you or other members are discussing your business and ideas, make sure the parties who are present sign a non-disclosure agreement drafted by an attorney. You might not get it, but just the act of asking shows that you are to be taken seriously.

Calculated Risk – Doing business with a friend or someone who can't afford to lose is a risk. This can take many forms, such as an up-and-coming singer/songwriter who is positive that his brother-in-law, currently a manager at the local movie theater, is the perfect person to manage his career. This is just a suggestion, but one with which many people would agree – avoid doing business with your friends. Even if lawyers are involved, it has a tendency to get messy very quickly. If someone can't afford to lose a portion of their purse, chances are you will be the one losing a lot more.

Only One Plan – This might be the opposite of what you would like to be making plans about concerning your business, but you need to plan for more than just success. To be successful you must take into consideration the fact that it will be a bumpy road. You must remain flexible with your business plan and adapt it if necessary. Make plans for any issues or obstacles you can think of, and develop easy-to-understand contingency plans. Make sure all members and employees are aware of these so that things go as smoothly as possible.

Separation – This is something that is commonly overlooked but that can be an issue for LLCs, especially sole-member LLCs. Money starts coming in when profits are made, and if you are not careful, it is easy to mix your personal and business bank accounts. This issue usually arises due to time management or just convenience, but try your best to avoid making this mistake. Should something happen, it will become more difficult for creditors to distinguish between what is personal and what belongs to the business.

Employee Agreement – This is different from an operating agreement because it is not only for the members. This agreement is primarily for those LLCs that have employees, and it is incredibly important. You must have a standard agreement for all employees and consultants that cover issues such as confidentiality and ownership. The agreement will probably not seem all that crucial early on, but you will see its importance if a competitor poaches an employee. Keep in mind, too, that hiring someone from a company that has followed this step means that you must follow their previous employer's employee agreement; not doing so can cause problems.

Equal Partnerships – If you plan to form a multi-member LLC, keep in mind that a 50/50 split is going to be incredibly difficult. If each member's opinion carries equal weight, trouble will often follow. Surprisingly, it is not usually the big decisions that cause problems, but the small ones, such as the font of a logo. This can spiral out of control when emotional attachment and ego get in the way. You can still choose to go with an even split, but just know that it can be difficult to settle a dispute.

Operating Agreement

You know how important an operating agreement is. It can set the tone for your entire business and either make your life easier or more difficult. If a member has a question, the first place they should look is the operating agreement; hopefully, they will find the answer there. That is how detailed it should be. The operating agreement is the first stop for answers and to avoid issues. Keep that in mind when it is being drafted. Here is a list of things to consider when you draft your operating agreement.

Explain how to resolve disputes if there are an even number of members and an even split.

If a member chooses to retire or becomes incapacitated, how will their interest be valued and paid out?

Create a detailed plan for how salary and profits will be distributed. Do your research or consult a professional because depending on what type of business you have, there could be a formula to help.

Should a member be sued, will the LLC pay the legal fees? This has been an issue for many LLCs in the past and the operating agreement should definitely address it.

Label the business specifically; if it is an LLC, say so.

Include when and how a member can transfer their interest to someone else, or if they can use it as collateral on a loan.

One of the most common mistakes people make when it comes to an operating agreement is putting too much stock into a premade template. A quick internet search provides hundreds of free operating agreement templates. Although these might be a good start, they will not be enough. Your business is unique and your operating agreement should reflect this.

If you choose to do the whole thing by yourself, take your time. Think of every possible question and answer it in your operating agreement. Sleep on it, then reread everything and see if there is anything you missed. Look up and read other operating agreements online so you have an idea of what you're missing. There is no reason to rush, as this is an incredibly important document. It must be fretted over, read, and then reread. Note that it is so much more cost-effective to hire an attorney to look over the operating agreement at the beginning than to pay legal fees later should something go wrong.

Not all states require an operating agreement, but this does not mean you don't need one. It is still a very good idea to draft one, as it will clarify issues for you and the other members. Some people think that because their state does not require an operating agreement, there is no reason for them to have one. However, experts say that this is certainly not the case. It would be like a teacher attempting to teach a class without a syllabus – it is possible, but it will be messy and emotionally draining. There is no reason to do this to yourself, so be as prepared as possible and write the best operating agreement you possibly can.

Chapter 5

10 Steps to Forming Your LLC

Organizing your first LLC probably feels overwhelming, but if you break it down, it is really just a series of small, easy tasks. This chapter will explain each step, making it easier for you to start your LLC and take the path toward becoming a successful business owner. This way, you are not faced with the giant undertaking of starting a business from the ground up. If you are considering starting an LLC, you probably already have an idea of what the LLC will do, so that is taken care of. Now it is time for you to do the busy work that will form the actual LLC. Feel free to focus on one step at a time and work at your own pace. This is meant to make it feel a little more achievable and less daunting.

Step 1: Where to Organize?

Your LLC will be considered alive as soon as you and the other owners properly file the articles of organization with either a state's secretary or a similar department. Some states require you to file in other areas. The federal government does not charter any LLCs.

This will help you decide when to file:

- Know in what state or states you plan to operate the LLC.

- There will be filing fees. So, that you are not blindsided when someone asks you for money, know that each state sets its own fees.

- You will need to tend to filing fees and certain reports annually. Again, each state is different so make sure you do your research and know exactly what is expected of you when you file.

- Learn what advantages, such as privacy, you'll receive based on the specific state in which you file.

In general, if your LLC will be relatively small and will operate in only one state, you need to organize and register your LLC in that state. However, if you plan to operate in more than one state, you will need to register your LLC in each of the states in which you plan to operate. Some states will require you to register your LLC as a guest and, of course, you will be responsible for all necessary fees. For example, if you want your LLC to be registered in Tennessee and do business in Delaware, you will need to register your LLC in Delaware as well as Tennessee, paying the filing fees for both states.

Picking the location where you form your LLC can be as complicated as choosing the best legal structure. However, you have two choices as to where you register: either domestic or foreign. If you opt for domestic filing, your LLC will conduct business in the same state in which it is registered. However, if you file foreign, you free up your LLC to do business in other states so long as it is registered in those states as well.

Any LLC that conducts its business outside of the states of its registration will be required to file what is called a "foreign qualification." This allows the LLC to do business in other states. Some things to take into consideration when deciding how to file include the additional paperwork, tax treatments, and compliance or disclosure obligations.

Many LLC owners decide to file their LLCs as domestic in their home states because this is the most logical choice if most of their business comes from the same state. An example would be if you are running a clothing store and most of your sales come from your home state; in this case, the best thing to do is file and register in that state. If you choose to file your LLC in a different state, you will be paying additional fees associated with a foreign LLC.

Just as with other businesses, you will be required to abide by both local and state laws, and pay both local and state taxes and additional fees. You will also face additional complexities, such as costs and paperwork involved in complying with mandates from other states. If it is not absolutely necessary to file as a foreign LLC, filing as a domestic LLC is the most cost effective and easy way to go.

Some new LLCs have plans to conduct business in multiple states other than their own. If this describes you, your LLC should definitely be filed as foreign. Also, it would be a great idea and in your best interest to consult with a tax professional or lawyer to determine whether filing as a foreign LLC is really the best course of action for both you and the other members. Three states stand out as having especially good reputations for being conducive locations for a foreign LLC.

Delaware – In general, Delaware has a reputation for being incredibly business friendly; more than half of all publicly traded companies and around 63 percent of all Fortune 500 companies were incorporated in this state. The statutes governing the creation of LLCs are accommodating and progressive, and they require cheaper filing fees. For foreign LLCs that do business in Delaware, no corporate income taxes are levied, and franchise taxes in Delaware are relatively low. There is no need to fulfill residency mandates to register your LLC, and you can also reap the benefits of Delaware's reportorial requirements and limited disclosure laws.

Delaware also has a separate and special court dedicated to only business-related cases; it has more than two centuries of experience settling business disputes and interpreting laws that dictate business activities. Their Division of Corporations is also known to offer very fast customer service.

Nevada – This is another state with laws and a judicial system that are favorable to businesses. Nevada does not have franchise taxes, corporate income taxes, or personal income taxes, and the state itself does not share information with the IRS. If you are an LLC owner in Nevada, you get the benefit of not being named in public registration filings of your LLC. This is an example of a state that does not require an operating agreement.

Wyoming – As with the other two states, Wyoming is considered business friendly. The state requires very little reporting, and mandatory annual meetings can be held outside the state. Just like Nevada, there are no personal, franchise, or corporate income taxes. Wyoming maintains the added perk of privacy since you are not identified as the owner of your LLC in public records. In addition, Wyoming offers lifetime proxies, which helps you protect your identity and assets by allowing other people to hold and exercise the obligations that come with being a member while you keep control of your voting rights.

Step 2: Naming

Now is a good time to choose your LLC's name. Keep in mind that you can use a different trade name in the market; it does not have to be the name of your LLC. Using different names for business and trade is known as doing business as a fictitious name. For instance, a store is called

Vitalift while the LLC's registered business name is Vitamin Lifting Systems Limited Liability Company. Your biggest worry from a legal standpoint is making sure you do not choose the name of another business or person. This means that your company name cannot infringe on another service mark or trademark rights. If you fail to ensure this, you can find yourself in a lot of legal trouble. Also, remember that the secretary of your chosen state will not allow an LLC to use a name that has already been taken, but the secretary has information about only that particular state. If you want to make sure your name is unique, you will need to do your homework when it comes to the other states in which you operate; do not rely solely on your chosen state's secretary.

Your LLC's name must incorporate identifiers, such as Limited Liability Company, LLC, or Limited Liability Co. Keep this in mind when you are filing, as forgetting it will hinder your progress. Some states do not require such identifiers to be in the name, but some do. Remember that this does not have to be the name of the business to which the public is exposed, so it does not have to be catchy. The name must simply comply with the laws in whatever state you are registering the LLC.

Step 3: Registered Agent

A registered agent is a person or business that your LLC can authorize and obligate to receive legal documents on its behalf. An LLC is not a physical, real person; it would be impossible for it to be served legal documents, so that is where a registered agent comes into play. Your LLC's registered agent should be identified in the articles of organization. You can replace your registered agent by filing a notice with the state's secretary; this is done for many reasons, so don't worry if you must switch. Some states might use a different term to refer to registered agents, so make sure you include this as part of your research into the state in which you wish to register.

Your LLC's agent can be almost anyone, such as yourself, a designated officer, another member, a lawyer, a family friend, or any person or company that provides professional registered agent services. The agent's name must be publicly recorded, so if you prefer to be anonymous, choose a professional registered agent instead of yourself. The registered agent must have a valid physical address in the same state where you will register your LLC. If your LLC will not operate in the state where it is registered, you will need to have a registered agent in the state where you organized the LLC. Keep in mind that there are many additional expenses related to this, so it is usually in people's best interest to organize in the same state in which the business operates.

Using a professional lawyer or firm as a registered agent has benefits, as they will be well-versed in most of the documents that will be served to the LLC. They will also be responsible for important federal and state-related documents such as tax forms, annual reports, legal notices, and the like. If you do not choose a registered agent wisely, you run the risk of not receiving legal documents in a timely manner or at all, or of having them dealt with improperly. This should not be a risk you take in regards to your business.

Registered Agent Qualifications

- Physically present and available at the LLC's office on a regular basis to retrieve or receive legal documents that might have been delivered there.

- Understand the compliance and business entity rules in the specific state in which the LLC operates.

- A good understanding of all business types, such as LLCs, corporations, and partnerships.

- Able to use monitoring tools and services.

- Be up to date on new compliance procedures, telling others immediately when they are issued.

- Able to tell the members immediately if their good standing with the authorities has changed and why so that any problems can be handled as quickly as possible.

- Monitor and track other states' changes or developments in their compliance events.

- Tell members if there are any general changes of which they must be aware.

A registered agent will be of great value when it comes to annual reports as if your LLC does not file its reports on time and properly, its good standing could be jeopardized. A good registered agent will prevent that from happening by knowing exactly when and what to file. Some people stress themselves out and work themselves to the bone trying to understand and do their own work in addition to the work a registered agent would do. There is a simple solution to this: hire a registered agent. It might seem expensive, but think about how much stress it will save you. Sometimes it is important to do what is best for you and the LLC.

Step 4: Organization

This is the time when you begin the actual creation process. You must decide whether you plan to organize your LLC by yourself, seek help from a discount limited liability service company, or hire a lawyer. Each of the three approaches has its own benefits and drawbacks.

Self-organization

This option will obviously save you the most money because you are not paying someone else to do the dirty work for you. However, unless you are an expert on this topic or have a lot of experience with it, you might end up spending more money down the road when you are attempting to fix problems or address complications that arise due to sloppy organization. For example, if you incorrectly or carelessly organized your LLC, you might not be able to enjoy the limited liability protection a well-organized LLC gives its members. This means that your LLC's creditors might be able to pursue your personal assets as settlement for the LLC's unpaid debts.

Discount LLC Organization Services

This is a better approach compared to the DIY method mentioned above, but it will cost more. Using services like these will cost around $300, but you will encounter a fluid and competent LLC organizing process and services. Firms like these can file your LLC's articles of organization with the correct department or office. They will also handle the creation of your LLC's boilerplate operating agreement. In addition, these types of firms will take minutes during your LLC's first membership meeting.

These organizations can be valuable for the money. They are convenient and they will take care of the hassles and technicalities of dealing with different states. There is also the knowledge that your LLC's organization has been handled correctly and faster than if you had done it yourself. However, remember that such businesses provide these services often and for many different LLCs, so the minutes and boilerplate agreement might not be easy to understand if you are new to the business.

Business Attorney

The last option is to hire a lawyer to help with the organization of your LLC. Attorneys will provide you with many different services, including:

Solutions and alternatives to improve your organizing success.

Assistance with the technical and complex parts of organizing your LLC, like the operating agreement.

Proactive management of potential risks and situations your LLC could face depending on the market in which it is participating.

Ensuring that your LLC complies with laws and regulations, especially in terms of raising capital for your LLC.

The cost of hiring a lawyer varies drastically, but generally, they cost between $100 and $400 an hour. This option is quite a bit more expensive, but you can assume that the more expensive attorneys will provide the best quality of service.

Step 5: LLC Ownership

Your LLC will need to distribute shares of ownership, called "units," to you and the other members. This serves as an integral part of its organization. Each member's units in the LLC are collectively called their percentage of ownership or interest in the LLC. For instance, if your LLC will give 100 units to you and the other members, and you are given 70 of those units, your interest or percentage of ownership is 70 percent. Your LLC must do this from the very start; you should not proceed with filing the articles of organization until this course has been completed.

One of the biggest rights each member has is the right to vote. However, the extent of a member's voting power depends on how much of the LLC they own or have an interest in. Let's use the same example; you own 70 units, which means that you, as a member, have 70 votes out of 100. More units or a higher percentage of ownership mean more control within the LLC. In this example, you would control the company, since you have the majority share and votes.

Members

When LLCs were first introduced in the United States, states urged them to include multiple members, meaning that single-member LLCs were not allowed. For many people's sake, it is fortunate that this is no longer the case, as all states now allow single-member LLCs. On the other hand, there is no limit to how many members your LLC can have. You and the other members have the power to set the limit on how many members the LLC can have. Yet while you can admit as many members as you choose, the adage "the more, the merrier" does not always apply here. There are some cases, such as with equity financing, in which more is better, but there are also times when less is more.

Every member, including you, must provide an investment representation letter. This gives the LLC a good level of assurance that the member is qualified and fit to be a member. In this letter, the member will also need to disclose their objectives for investing in the LLC. This is done in accordance with the securities laws of the federal and state governments.

It is possible for members to contribute to the LLC in the form of non-cash assets like services, property, or receivables. The monetary value of these types of contributions will determine how much ownership or interest that particular member has in the LLC. These values must be determined and agreed upon early in the planning stage to prevent complications and issues in the future. The operating agreement should contain a detailed area dedicated to the monetary values of contributions.

Step 6: Filing the Articles of Organization

This step gives your LLC life! It is usually just a single-page document that outlines the following:

- Name of the LLC

- Registered agent's name and address for purposes of receiving legal documents on behalf of the LLC

- A statement including your LLC's reason for existence or purpose

- Appropriate names, such as other members, managers, or designated officers

- Expected life, such as whether the LLC will be dissolved on a particular date or continue indefinitely

As you have already learned, your LLC starts to come to life when the articles of organization are filed with the secretary or appropriate department. Remember that there will be a fee involved and without that fee being paid, your LLC will have no chance to come to life.

In most instances, the LLC's initial members or chosen managers don't have to be assigned immediately to the articles of organization unless the state in which you're organizing your LLC requires that this is included. This is just another reason why the DIY approach might not be the best choice for you. However, if you insist, do your research or hire an expert to handle it for you. You could be in a situation in which you have organized an LLC in one state, but because each state has different laws and regulations, if you tried the same thing in another state, you would be considered a rookie.

Your LLC's additional members and managers can easily be elected after filing. Articles of organization are thought of as documents of public nature, meaning that any citizen of that state can look them up. This limits privacy since strangers can learn the names and even addresses of the registered agents, so take that into consideration when creating your LLC.

Nearly every website of the office of every state's secretary provides a sample or template of the articles of organization. This can be extremely helpful since it is issued by that particular state and will cut down on the hassle and time involved in finding the correct format for the articles of organization.

Step 7: LLC Kit

Your LLC's kit is just a binder that will hold important documents like the articles of organization, the operating agreement, meeting minutes, the membership log, licenses, and tax filings. The kit can cost between $50 and $100 and normally includes:

- Stock certificate forms

- LLC embossed seal

- Empty transfer and membership logs

- Template or sample of minutes, the operating agreement, and the organizational meeting structure

Federal and state laws do not require you to have these kits; they are entirely optional but incredibly helpful. Since you are going to be preparing and filling extremely important documents for your LLC, you might as well take advantage of such kits, which make it easier for you to prepare, file, and organize all the important documents you will come across.

LLC Seal

Your LLC's seal is an embossing seal that is manually operated. It will emboss your LLC's name, its operating or organizing state, and its organization date. The LLC seal is closely related to the corporate seal. It was once required for all LLCs in every state, but now it is usually not required. Again, check with your state, because each is different.

Stock Certificates

These are printed, tangible documents that show a member's ownership of units in an LLC. Most LLC kits contain blank versions of these that you can use to make your own. You can manually print the necessary details on your LLC's certificates, for example, by using a typewriter or putting them through a printer.

Historically, stock certificates were connected to only corporations. Today, they are also used for

LLCs even though they tend to operate with much less formality and complications as compared to a corporation. While LLCs do not normally use stock certificates, you can still use them, as they give members written, tangible evidence of their ownership or interest in the LLC.

Membership Ledger

This is just a log or table that shows the current owners or members of the LLC, as well as their respective ownership percentage in relation to the total. When new members are added, usually by purchasing an existing member's interests or shares in the LLC, the log or ledger should be updated to reflect any changes in the LLC's ownership. It should also show the reduced shares of the members from whom the new members purchased their shares or interests. This should be very thorough, so any member can look back at it and immediately understand who has how much interest in the LLC, both old and new.

It is basically impossible to exaggerate the importance of the membership log or ledger; your LLC must be very consistent and diligent in keeping it updated. Consider the log or ledger as your deed or title to a property, meaning that it is the primary evidence of interest or ownership in your LLC. It can even be used to settle ownership disputes in court. To minimize confusion and possible negative outcomes, it is a good idea to give updated copies of the log or ledger to the LLC's members.

Step 8: Management

The next step in the process is to decide whether your LLC will be managed by its members or by a professional manager. If the LLC will be managed by members, it is known as member-managed; if it will be managed by an outside employee, it is known as manager-managed. Your choice of management structure will not be permanent because your LLC can, with no restrictions other than those that you and the members place on it, change management styles from one to the other. Generally, all it takes for this to happen is a membership vote followed by an amendment or revision of the LLC's operating agreement.

Essentially, you and the other members are free to run and operate your LLC like a partnership if you choose to have it be member-managed. Mostly, smaller LLCs are member-managed because there is no need to select managers or have a formal vote. In addition, almost all single-member LLCs are member-managed for this same reason. This is also the most cost-effective option, especially in the beginning.

Making your LLC a manager-managed one means that you must appoint professional managers to run it like a corporation or a limited partnership. This can make life less stressful for you and the other members because you will not have to control and direct daily operations, but it can also complicate both your life and the other members' lives in a different way. For instance, there must be a formal vote when appointing or removing managers. You will also have to come up with guidelines that govern these activities. Typically, large LLCs are manager-managed because of their size and the complexity of their business activities, as well as their larger wallets.

If you and the other members decide to be a manager-managed LLC, you will need to create strict rules at the onset. One of these rules involves the number of professional managers you will hire; the larger your LLC, the more managers you will need. Decide whether to hire an odd or even number of managers; in general, odd-numbered management teams are the preference because this eliminates the possibility of a deadlock during the decision-making process.

Once you and your members decide on a management structure, as well as how many managers you are going to hire, you will need to choose the best provision for your operating agreement. If your LLC is to be a manager-managed one, your operating agreement must identify your initial set of managers; therefore, you will need to choose and hire them.

When all is said, and done, the managers you choose should be at the service of you and the other members. Make sure the operating agreement includes clear and specific provisions for managing managers, especially when it comes to replacing them if they are not performing up to standard. Some experts say that it is a good idea to rotate or change your managers every so often, perhaps every other year or so. This is recommended because indefinite appointments can lead to issues such as familiarity, complacency, or even a sense of entitlement.

Step 9: Operating Agreement

Your LLC's operating agreement is the basis for how the LLC will conduct business. The operating agreement includes factors like how meetings will be conducted, how voting procedures will be conducted, what constitutes a "quorum," and the rights and powers of members and managers. Generally, operating agreements are between five and 25 pages; if you don't know where to start, the LLC kit can be incredibly helpful because it provides a sample or template. The operating agreement does not need to be filed with your LLC's state of organization or operations. The operating agreement is confidential and makes up a large part of your LLC's important documents or records.

You and the other members will need to work together and spend some time on coming up with a very good operating agreement. Even if you are being guided by a template, it is still only a sample, so make sure that you add all the important things that make your LLC unique. Make sure that before enforcing and finalizing it, all members, including you, have read through it completely and carefully, and understand every part of it fully. It is much easier to make changes to it when it is still being drafted rather than in the future. Once it is set, you will need a formal vote to make changes to it.

Even if the state in which you registered does not require you to have an operating agreement, it is not wise to operate an LLC without one. One of the reasons for this is that if agreements are not documented, they can be left open to misrepresentations and misunderstandings because there is no objective or documentary evidence that can settle disputes. When you have a formal operating agreement, disagreements and disputes are kept to a minimum since there is so little room for subjectivity.

If the members choose not to use an operating agreement, the particular state's default rules and regulations, which are in every state's statutes, will govern the limited liability company. Of course, these rules do not cover every possible situation that could arise; they just touch on the basics. Therefore, it is not wise to rely on the default regulations because chances are they will not be the right ones for your company.

Also, using an operating agreement can help protect the members from personal liability in terms of the business. Members should know and try to give the LLC a separate existence; the LLC should be held out to the public. An LLC without a formally written operating agreement will seem more like a sole proprietorship or a partnership, which do not have the same level of protection as an LLC. Limited liability companies require fewer formalities than do corporations, but that does not mean they require none at all.

Percentage of Ownership

One of the most difficult and important decisions owners and members face is how to divide the ownership percentages among the members. This is a time to choose carefully. In most cases, more than 50 percent of the vote of an LLC's members can dictate major decisions within the company. This is the main reason why company founders try to keep 51 percent ownership. Also, if the limited liability company is ever sold, the money from the sale will be divided among the owners in proportion to their ownership percentage. Each member's percentage of ownership should be written down in the operating agreement. This should reduce the chances of misunderstandings or issues related to the share of ownership.

Distributive Share

The distributive share is the owner's percentage share of the LLC's losses and profits. This will usually equal their percentage of ownership shares. This is how most people set up their LLCs. For instance, imagine that Kelly has 65 percent ownership and John has 35 percent ownership. At the end of the year, their profits are $20,000, which will be divided between the two of them as owners. They will divide the profits based on the ownership share, so Kelly will receive 65 percent of the profits, or $13,000, leaving John with 35 percent, or $7,000.

A good operating agreement will include the following:

- Powers and expected duties of members and managers

- Time and date of the annual meetings that managers and members will attend

- Process of removing a manager, if needed

- Procedure for electing or appointing a manager

- Minimum requirements for member/manager votes

- Technique for voting with written consent, but without being physically present at a formal meeting

- Giving proxy to the other members

- Dividing losses and profits among the members

- Rules defining the procedures for transferring shares when a member wants to sell their interest

The members of the company will adopt the agreement by signing it and agreeing that it will run the operation. An operating agreement is a contract among the members of the company; once it has been enforced, the limited liability company's members must comply with its terms.

Step 10: Tax ID Number

Since an LLC is a legal entity, the federal government demands that it have its own Federal Employer Identification Number or FEIN. In addition, most banks will require that you have a FEIN before you can open a bank account for the LLC.

First, go to the IRS website, IRS.gov, and type "EIN" in the search box. This will bring up a link that asks you to "Apply Online Now." Click on the link; this will redirect you to another page that will show you how to get your FEIN. On that same page, you can click on the button that says "Begin Application." Make sure you click on the section that says "Limited Liability Company" and, when you are prompted, choose your business structure. Fill out the rest of the questions, answering honestly.

Next, you can call the IRS at 800-829-4933; pay attention to the menu and choose to speak to someone about business taxes. Make sure you keep your LLC's information near you so that you can easily answer any questions. The representative will ask for a name, address, and social security number. After all of this is confirmed in the system and you are verified, your LLC will receive its FEIN, which can be used immediately for business purposes.

Now download Form S-4 from the IRS website and print it out. Only after the form is printed can the information be written on it. This form must also be signed by your LLC's authorized representative, which can be you, another member, or the manager. Once you have filled out the form, fax it to 859-669-5760. You will also need to provide the IRS with a return fax number because that is how the IRS will send you the FEIN.

Something to remember is that LLCs must have the same fiscal year-end as the rest of the members. A person's fiscal year ends on December 31; therefore, so does the LLC's, making taxes due by April 15 of the following year.

Now you have a good understanding of everything that goes into forming an LLC. You know what to do, as well as what not to do. There is nothing wrong with taking your time and making sure you absorbed what you read. This will help you be a successful business owner. Remember that not all LLCs are the same and there is nothing wrong with that. That is the beauty of an operating agreement; it can be tweaked and adjusted if necessary.

Chapter 6

Converting a Different Business Entity to an LLC

This book might have inspired you to jump on the LLC bandwagon before your partnership or sole proprietorship gets into trouble and suddenly your savings dry up. It is possible to make the switch; it just takes some time and effort.

Sole Proprietorship

If you would like to transform your sole proprietorship into a single-member LLC, the process is generally straightforward. All your business assets should already be in your name, so you will simply transfer them to your LLC in exchange for your own membership interest in your LLC. Most states allow for the creation of single-member LLCs, but some do not, so make sure it is a possibility for you.

If you must have at least one partner to form an LLC, consider getting a minority partner or a friend or relative who will own only two to four percent of the LLC. You do not need to distribute any profits to this person if you choose not to. They are basically a silent partner.

When you transfer your assets into the LLC, it is considered a non-taxable event, which means you will not be taxed on the value of your sole proprietorship's assets. This is a great thing. The trickiest part of this in terms of taxes is transferring what is called "recourse debt," which is business debt for which the owner is personally liable. However, once that debt is converted into the LLC, it will be protected; therefore, the IRS requires you to pay taxes on it. This debt transfer is treated as though it is a cash distribution. If your previous sole proprietorship had business liabilities that you had personally guaranteed, the value of those will be taxed when you form the LLC. If you think this will create a rather large tax burden, seek help from a professional accountant. They have ways to minimize or completely avoid these kinds of scenarios.

Partnership

Going from a partnership to an LLC is also relatively easy because they have identical tax structures. The only difference, really, is that in an LLC you and the other members will be protected from personal liability. All partners must transfer the business assets they own into the LLC. By doing this, they gain membership in the newly formed LLC. Before continuing, you must make sure all the partners agree to the conversion. This transfer of assets is also tax free. When transferring over recourse debt, be careful; just like with the sole proprietorship, the IRS will consider this transfer a taxable cash distribution.

Corporations

Some corporations provide liability protection and are useful for raising capital from investors, but that can create tax problems for developing businesses that see their corporation's profits taxed twice – first when it is initially made and second when it is distributed. According to section 721 of the Internal Revenue Code, corporations can transfer property to an LLC without having to pay any taxes on it, just as an individual can. Assets that a corporation holds and that have appreciated over time will not be taxed based on their higher value. These assets will be seen as having kept their original value, but they will be taxable when they are sold back into the market.

It is easy for things to get confusing and complicated when transferring assets into an LLC. The federal paperwork is notoriously complicated, and even if you do manage to get through it, you will still have to complete the state and local paperwork. This often results in unforeseen tax requirements, which can slow the process immensely. It might actually be cheaper and easier to process your conversion as a merger with the LLC instead of a conversion, leaving the LLC as the surviving entity. The other option is to do a "statutory conversion," which is when a corporation is not legally dissolved before it is converted into an LLC.

Some corporations found that a dual-entity strategy best met their needs. This is when both the corporation and the LLC continue to exist, but the LLC leases assets from the corporation. This can be incredibly beneficial for an LLC because it does not need to buy everything it needs; leasing is usually cheaper. To learn more about these options and to make sure they fit within the laws of a specific state, you will want to seek the help of an accountant, who can look at your corporation's books and tell you what your options are and how to achieve them.

Even if converting does not suit your needs today, don't ignore the potential value that restructuring can provide. The needs of a business change frequently, especially with technology, trends, and fads. That said, it is important to consider restructuring if it might benefit the business. The market is a complex and dynamic place; just because something isn't working today doesn't mean it won't work tomorrow.

Other Books by Elliot J. Smith

Available at the Kindle Store

Information at http://amzn.to/2koxLgY

Robert's Rules: The Ultimate Guide to
Understanding and Practicing Robert's Rules of
Order

Business Plan: How to Write a Business Plan –
Template and Examples Included!

Passive Income: Four Beginner & Advanced
Business Models to Start Creating Passive Income
Online

Lightning Source UK Ltd.
Milton Keynes UK
UKOW06f2034141117
312754UK00005B/163/P

9 781542 864626